Contents

IN THE GARAGE

Engines rev, tools clink and clang, machines hum and buzz, couriers drop off packages, the smell of oil and grease hangs in the air — it's another busy day in the garage.

This car's been serviced and is ready to be picked up.

Motor vehicle servicing and repairs has changed in recent years. New vehicles are fitted with sophisticated computer-controlled systems and in modern workshops, electronic diagnostic equipment is used to find faults. Large service departments use the latest computers. But it's also important to be able to work on the older cars as well.

Hi – I'm Joe. I'm doing an Advanced Apprenticeship in a local garage, learning to work with a variety of light vehicles – mostly private cars.

I have always had an interest in cars and, after I finished my GCSEs, was lucky enough to get into training through an Apprenticeship. At first, it all seemed quite strange – very different from school. And there was so much to remember! But everyone was very friendly, and they explained what the training would involve.

I've learnt how to do the basic servicing which all vehicles need – from changing the oil to fitting new brake pads. Sometimes it gets really busy, especially if a job ends up taking much longer than expected. Planning your work is very important – customers get upset if their vehicles aren't ready when they come to collect them!

As part of my training, I also go to college one day a week, and I'm working towards NVQ level 3. I enjoy college, although the work is more demanding than I expected. At college I can spend time with other students of my age but at the garage I'm the youngest by far.

I'd like to get more qualifications and work my way up to eventually having my own business!

Sunday's my favourite day!

We've got a lot on this week.

UNDER THE HOOD

Just like people, cars need regular check-ups, known as a service, to make sure they are running properly.

All cars need to be serviced at regular intervals, according to instructions set out by the vehicle's manufacturers. Servicing involves making routine checks, finding faults or problems, overhauling or replacing worn or faulty parts and using special equipment and road tests to make sure the vehicle performs as it should.

When a car comes into the garage, I inspect the engine and follow a checklist to look over important mechanical parts for wear and tear.

old sports car in for repair

checking the oil level

Oil is essential for the smooth running of a car's engine.

Joe gets his hands dirty fixing this car's brakes.

CHECKLIST

- ☑ belts
- ☑ hoses
- ☑ plugs
- ☑ brakes
- ☑ fuel systems
- ☑ electrics — lights, wipers, heater, dash indicators etc.
- ☑ tyres

Fixing car brakes is a very important job.

cam belt on a four cylinder engine

4TH SERVICE MAINTENANCE RECORD

- ☑ replace engine oil and filter
- ☑ replace engine coolant
- ☑ replace spark plugs
- ☑ replace air filter
- ☑ tighten drive shaft bolts

removing a dirty air filter

Sean prefers to keep his hands clean while changing spark plugs.

INSPECT THE FOLLOWING

- ☑ drive belts
- ☑ battery
- ☑ brake pedal, parking brake
- ☑ brake pads / discs
- ☑ power steering fluid
- ☑ brake pipes / hoses
- ☑ steering wheel / linkage
- ☑ drive shaft boots
- ☑ ball joints, dust covers
- ☑ automatic transaxle fluid
- ☑ tyres, lights, horn, wipers, washers
- ☑ air conditioner
- ☑ road test vehicle

Road testing cars is fun, especially when it's a nice sports car!

km/h

140
160
180
200
220
240
260

DIDYOUKNOW?

SPEEDOMETER

The speedometer dial on the dashboard lets the driver know how fast the car is going. A speedometer instrument is attached to one of the wheels — the faster the wheel's speed, the higher the speedometer reading.

A SICK CAR

I often work on cars that aren't running properly and no-one knows why. Firstly, I talk to the vehicle's owner about the car's symptoms and then take it for a test drive so I can get a feel for how it's running. Using a checklist, I eliminate the simple things that might be causing the problem.

After discovering the problem, I repair the damage to get the car back on the road again.

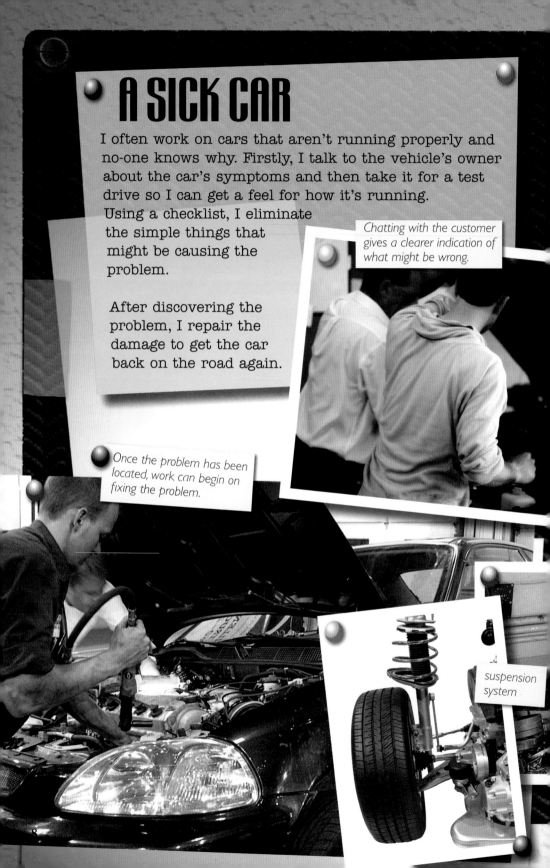

Chatting with the customer gives a clearer indication of what might be wrong.

Once the problem has been located, work can begin on fixing the problem.

suspension system

A smoking exhaust, loud, squeaky, shuddering brakes and a spluttering engine are all signs that a car needs a mechanic's attention — fast!

- A mechanic needs to know about all areas of car repair. However, in a large workshop, a mechanic can specialise in just one area.
- Automatic transmission technicians work on gear trains, hydraulic pumps and other parts of the transmission.
- Tune-up technicians adjust and replace timing belts, valves and spark plugs.
- Front-end mechanics align and balance wheels, and repair steering and suspension systems.
- Brake repairers adjust and replace brakes, brake linings and pads.

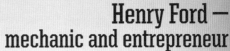
not a good sign

DID YOU KNOW?

Henry Ford — mechanic and entrepreneur

In 1903, American Henry Ford produced the Model A Ford. It was the first car designed to be built in large numbers. Ford had the idea of mass-producing a car and having it assembled along a production line. He formed the Ford Motor Company. His 1908 Model T Ford was the world's first mass-produced car built on a production line.

The light Model T Touring Car was introduced in October 1908. It was priced at US$825.

automatic transmission dismantled on a workbench

How do you become a motor mechanic?

Finding out how things work always fascinated me, and I like working with tools and my hands. Much to the horror of my parents, as a kid I loved pulling my bike apart and reassembling it — just to see if I could do it successfully. More often than not, I managed to get it running as good as new.

Repairing bicycles as a kid was one of my favourite hobbies.

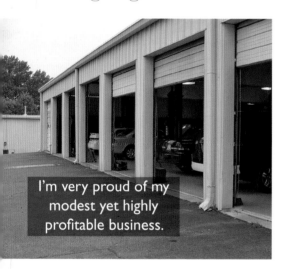

I'm very proud of my modest yet highly profitable business.

I did work experience at a local garage while I was still at school. I had to work hard to get the grades I needed in my English, maths and science GCSEs. When I finished school, I started an Advanced Apprenticeship as a light vehicle mechanic at the same garage. The apprenticeship was a combination of on-the-job training and a course at a training centre.

After I successfully completed my apprenticeship, I worked for a number of small, and large, garages until I finally set up my own business.

My garage is very busy, and I employ four full-time mechanics and one apprentice.

After school, there wasn't much time for fun and games because I'd head straight to the garage for work experience.

Entry to motor vehicle training is always competitive. You need to offer as high grades in GCSEs as possible, and to convince employers that you have a real interest in motor vehicle work. A course in vehicle maintenance will help to show your interest, and give you a chance to try it out. Tell prospective employers about anything mechanical you have done as a hobby.

OU CAN EITHER COMPLETE AN APPRENTICESHIP OR DO A LL TIME COLLEGE COURSE TO BECOME A MECHANIC.

motor mechanic apprenticeship has two parts:

N THE JOB RAINING

his provides you with the xperience of doing the job and orking in a real-life environment.

FF THE JOB TRAINING

You are trained in practical skills and study work-related subjects.

IMPORTANT SCHOOL SUBJECTS FOR BEING A MECHANIC:

Maths Science ICT English

DYOUKNOW?

e 14- to 16-year-olds may have the opportunity ake a Young Apprenticeship in the motor industry, nbining work experience with an employer with dy at school and college. If successfully completed, could lead on to a post-16 Apprenticeship. more information ask at your local nnexions/Careers Office.

ALL IN A DAY'S WORK

Here's a list of some of the things a motor mechanic may find themselves doing during the day:

Careful filing of customer jobs makes life easier.

Explaining what's involved and the cost to customers is an important part of the job.

◆ replacing worn parts
◆ tuning vehicles to regain their performance
◆ inspecting vehicles before they are put up for sale
◆ fitting accessories
◆ test-driving vehicles to make sure faults have been corrected
◆ document and record information
◆ inspect vehicles and, with extra training, issue MOT certificates.

◆ routine servicing – carrying out a range of basic tasks and checks, such as changing the oil, checking the brakes etc
◆ investigating problems reported by customers

tool set, tyre iron and jack stand — just some of the tools of the trade

Skilled technicians are in demand. Employers are keen to attract recruits, especially those with the potential to become highly-skilled technicians. There are plenty of opportunities for keen young men and women with the right abilities. Once qualified, you may be able to gain further specialised qualifications, such as those offered by vehicle manufacturers. It may even be possible to go on to a higher education course in automotive engineering.

You will need to be able to:

◆ understand how engines work
◆ use basic tools
◆ follow written instructions and read diagrams
◆ solve practical problems
◆ work with hi-tech electronic testing equipment
◆ communicate with customers and suppliers of parts
◆ plan and schedule your work
◆ cope with a busy workload.

Every car is made up of hundreds of parts, large and small, that all contribute to the car's performance, safety and handling.

The engine

Inside the engine are chambers called cylinders. Inside each cylinder is a piston that moves up and down. The piston starts at the top of the cylinder and moves down, drawing in a combination of air and fuel. The cylinder is then sealed, trapping the mixture inside.

spark plugs

The piston then moves back up, compressing the mixture. This compression makes the explosion more powerful.

When the piston reaches the top of its stroke, the spark plug emits a spark to ignite the fuel.

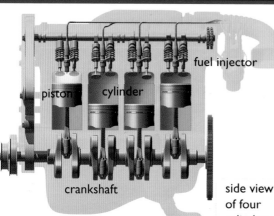

fuel injector

piston cylinder

crankshaft

side view of four cylinder car engine

car engine

FORMULA ONE

Formula One racing tyres are wide so that the car can go as fast as possible while maintaining stability on the road. They are made from very soft rubber which offers the best possible grip against the texture of the racetrack.

crankshaft

The petrol and air mixture explodes, driving the piston down with great force. This turns the crankshaft. As the crankshaft turns it makes the wheels go round and the car moves.

Once the piston is at the bottom again, the exhaust valve opens. The piston returns to the top, pushing the burned exhaust gas from the explosion out of the cylinder into the exhaust pipe.

And then the process repeats itself.

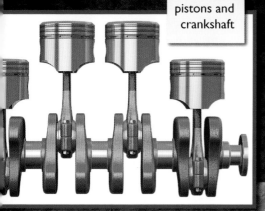

pistons and crankshaft

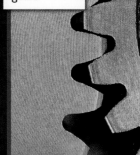

interlocking gears

The gears

Gears, or toothed wheels, are used to create forward or backward motion by interlocking two or more gears together. They are fixed to rods called shafts. These shafts turn when the interlocking gears rotate. The turning shafts then cause the wheels of a car to turn around. The bigger the gear wheel, the faster the shaft turns and the greater the speed of the car. Gears help the car to travel at different speeds.

Most cars have four or five gears. Some gears are for starting off and driving slowly, while others are for driving fast or reversing.

open gearbox showing gears in the foreground and driveshaft in the background

The fuel system

Fuel is stored in a tank. It is drawn to the engine by a pump. The pump sends fuel to a filter, which removes any unwanted particles. It is then introduced into the engine by a fuel injector. (Carburettors are still found in small engines and in older or specialised automobiles such as those designed for stock car racing. However, fuel injection is now more commonly used.)

When fuel is ignited in the engine's cylinders it explodes, creating waste gases. These gases travel along pipes from each engine cylinder to a front exhaust then along another pipe to a silencer box and finally out the rear exhaust. The silencer slows down the gases rushing out of the engine making it quieter.

filling the tank with petrol

Wheels

The wheel of a car is made up of five parts — the nuts and bolts, tyre, wheel rim, spring and hub cap. Nuts and bolts fix the wheel to the car's axle. The tyres are covered in patterns called tread that help the car grip the road. The wheel rim holds the tyre in place. The spring allows the wheel to bounce slightly on the ground's surface giving passengers a smoother ride. The hub cap is purely decorative — it covers all the nuts that attach the wheel to its axle.

The tread on tyres helps the car grip the road's surface — even when wet and slippery.

mechanic attaching wheel to car's axle

The brakes

rotor

Brakes slow the car down and make it stop. Each wheel has its own brake.

The brake pedal is connected to the brakes by pipes filled with a liquid called brake fluid. When the brake pedal is pressed, fluid is pumped out of a cylinder and along the pipes to the brakes. The pressure exerted by the brake fluid operates the brakes.

There are two types of brakes — disc brakes and drum brakes.

new rotor and caliper installed in a car

caliper

rotor

set of brake pads used in disc brakes

Disc brakes

Front wheels have disc brakes. Disc brakes consist of a rotor and a caliper. There are brake pads inside the caliper. When brake pressure is applied the brake pads grab both sides of the spinning rotor to slow the wheel.

Brake shoes slow the wheel by pressing the brake drum, creating friction.

Drum brakes

Drum brakes are often used in the back wheels. When brake pressure is applied, a set of shoes cause friction by pressing against the inner surface of a spinning drum. This stops the wheel turning.

Pressing the brake pedal activates the brakes.

brake drum

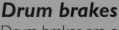

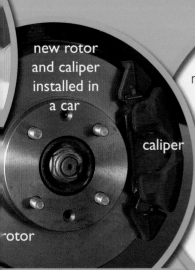

The steering

When the driver turns the steering wheel the front wheels turn, making the car go either left or right. The steering wheel is joined to a steering column, which is joined to a gear wheel called a pinion. When the pinion turns it makes a long bar, called a rack, move which directs the wheels.

steering wheel

rack and pinion

Electricity lights up the instruments at night.

Lights and electrics

Electricity powers the lights, spark plugs, sound system, heater, wipers, dash instruments and sometimes the windows. Lights are powered from a generator. When the engine is on it spins the generator around and as it spins the generator produces electricity. When the engine is turned off, electricity for the lights comes from the battery. The battery is recharged by the generator.

The primary function of the car battery is to start the engine.

Interior comfort and safety

Mechanics also check safety features like seats, seatbelts, driver airbags and anti-lock braking systems. An airbag is an inflatable pillow that can be stored in the instrument panel, side doors or the steering wheel. During a crash, the airbag inflates and absorbs the force of the driver and passengers as they are thrown around on impact. This decreases the chance of major injury.

Anti-locking braking systems (ABS) are important, because they allow the driver to keep steering when he or she has applied the brakes hard.

LEARNING ZONE
DEESIDE COLLEGE

TAKING CARE OF YOUR CAR

not something you want to see on the dashboard during a long trip

To prevent spending time on the side of the road, check the following before heading out on a long road trip:

- tyre tread and tyre pressure for good braking and handling
- engine oil
- water and radiator coolant levels
- petrol or diesel!

to prevent this happening …

UNLEADED FUEL ONLY

CHECK ENGINE

Do not attempt to take the radiator cap off when the engine is hot, because scalding coolant could spray out and burn you.

When the engine is cool, open the bonnet and check the coolant levels in the radiator. If coolant is needed, refill the radiator and drive to the nearest garage to check that everything is OK.

If the problem is not caused by low coolant levels, call for a breakdown service patrol officer, who can provide expert help.

What to do if your car overheats

Pull the car over to the side of the road and turn the engine off.

Wait for the engine to cool down — this could take about half an hour, depending on how long you've been driving and how hot the engine is.

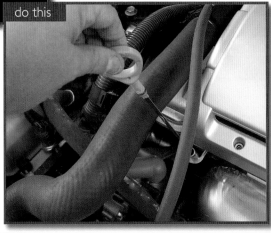
do this

Having your car serviced regularly ensures any problems are dealt with before they interfere with the car's smooth running.

General maintenance and upkeep tips

Check tyres are at the right pressure — this ensures they last longer and achieve better road grip.

Get your car serviced regularly.

checking air pressure

Keep you car clean and tidy — not only will it look good, but it will last longer.

CUSTOM CARS

Hot rods!

Custom car adapted for drag racing.

Custom cars are cars that have been specially adapted to the owner's personal style. People customise their cars by changing the tyres, working on the engine and lowering the frame within centimetres of the ground. Paint jobs and special interior features are also popular adaptations. In the end, the cars can look very different from how they started. Depending on the changes made, custom cars can become mean machines, street machines, muscle machines or hot rods! Racing custom cars is very popular.

FIXING PROBLEMS

What to do if you turn the key and nothing happens.

Check the fuel gauge on the dashboard to see if you have fuel (you'd be surprised how many people drive around on almost empty)!

Get a jump start!

Check to ensure the battery terminals are clean and tight.

Check the battery for power. If the lights, dashboard indicators or stereo are working you have power. If the lights are dim you may not have enough power to start the car. If this is the case, you'll need to recharge the battery.

If you have a flat battery, find someone with another car and some jump leads. Connect the jump leads up to both batteries, connecting positive to positive and negative to negative. Start the car with power and then start the car with the flat battery.

Let both cars run for around five minutes before you disconnect the jump leads. Take the flat battery for a drive to charge it up.

If the car still won't start — call for expert help.

It's a good idea to have a pair of jump leads in your car at all times.

How to change a tyre

Make sure you are off the road. Park on a safe, level surface. Ensure the car handbrake is on. Get the spare tyre, car jack and wheel brace out of the car. Firstly, remove the hub cap, then loosen the lug nuts in diagonal pairs using the wheel brace. (Removing and replacing the lug nuts in diagonal pairs keeps the wheel more stable while you are working.) Raise the car up with the car jack. Take the old tyre off and put on the new tyre. Put the lug nuts on and tighten them in diagonal pairs using the wheel brace. Let the jack down until the wheel is just touching the ground.

Tighten the lug nuts again to make sure they are secure. Finish lowering the vehicle and remove the jack. Put the tools and damaged tyre in the boot.

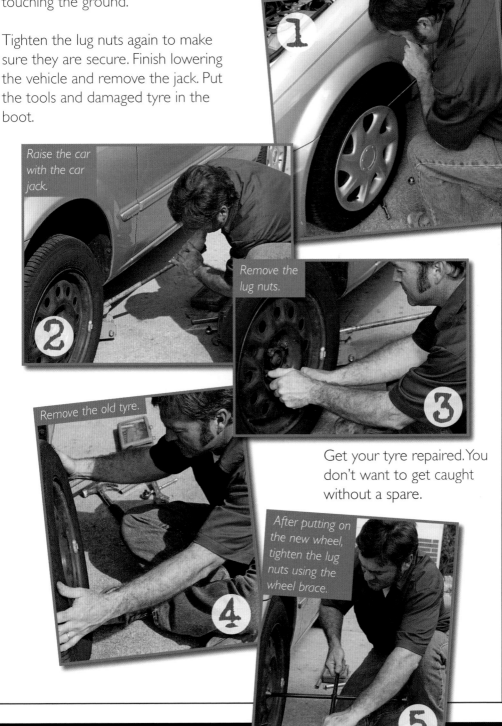

Remove the hub cap.

1

Raise the car with the car jack.

2

Remove the lug nuts.

3

Remove the old tyre.

4

Get your tyre repaired. You don't want to get caught without a spare.

After putting on the new wheel, tighten the lug nuts using the wheel brace.

5

COOL CARS

Cars are not just used for travel, they are also used for sport and fun.

Grand Prix racing began in France in 1894.

RACING CARS

Racing cars are built for maximum speed and the best possible road handling. Types of racing include Formula One, V8 Supercars, stock car, rally and drag.

Formula One

Formula One, also known as Grand Prix racing, is the fastest and most powerful kind of track racing. It is the highest class of car racing in the world. Cars can travel up to 320 km/h on straight sections of the track.

V8 engine

V8 Supercars

V8 Supercars racing is popular mainly in Australia and New Zealand. Normal cars are adapted for racing conditions.

Stock car racing

Stock car racing is popular in the USA. Stock cars are purpose-built racing cars that have the basic steel frame of a passenger car. Car speeds can reach up to 275 km/h.

stock car racing on an oval track

Rally car racing

Rally car driving is tough on cars. Rally racing is different from other forms of car racing because it takes place not on a circuit but on sand, mud and snow, all with many obstacles.

All cars follow the same route but start at different times. The course is divided into separate sections known as special stages. There is a time limit for each stage. The winner of the rally has the fastest overall time.

Drag racing

Drag racing involves starting from a dead stop and racing on a straight and level course of either 201 or 402 metres. Drag racing started in the USA and is now popular around the world.

Car racing is fun, but it can also be highly dangerous.

Rallying on dirt roads can get very messy!

warming up before a drag race

A very sharp bend on the Monaco Grand Prix Formula One circuit.

The driver usually waits in the car while the pit crew mechanics work.

Working on racing cars

Every race-car team has a group of dedicated mechanics who work long hours repairing, rebuilding, maintaining and servicing race cars between races.

car fuel gauge on full

E F

Between race meetings the cars are stripped, cleaned and repaired piece by piece as follows:

* all fuel and lubricants are drained and refilled
* brakes are removed and checked
* tyres are checked, flat spots are removed and wear is measured
* suspension is checked
* roll bar bearings and safety equipment is checked
* exhaust system is checked for cracks/damage
* engine and gearbox are removed for servicing
* damaged body panels are repaired.

Tools at the ready!

pulling in at the pit stop

Formula One racing is tough on the car.

Imagine being a mechanic in a racing car pit crew

The driver can feel that his tyres are wearing down. He radios ahead to the pit crew so you and the rest of the mechanics are ready when he pulls up. As a team, you race out to jack up the car, loosen the lug nuts, change the tyres and tighten the nuts again. You do it all in less than eight seconds!

It is also your job to use sign boards to let the driver know his position and how many laps are left in the race.

DID YOU KNOW?

Crowded pit stop!

On a Formula One pit stop there can be as many as 18 mechanics, each with a specific job to do. There are three people per wheel — one to remove the locking nut, one to remove the old tyre and a third to roll in the new tyre. Two people handle the fuelling rig, one person at each end operates the manual jack, one stands by the starter in case the engine stalls and another holds a sign paddle in front of the driver telling him when it is safe to go.

mechanics crowd round a racing car at the Formula One Grand Prix at the Bahrain International Circuit

AN IMPORTANT TOOL FOR RACE MECHANICS AND DRIVERS IS A DATA ACQUISITION SYSTEM

A data acquisition system lets both the driver and the mechanics know how the car is performing. It records and reports data while the car is being driven. The data is downloaded from the car to a laptop in the pit and is analysed after each session.

The system measures wheel speed, throttle position, steering angle, brake pressure and suspension. It also records engine oil pressure, oil temperature, water temperature, gearbox temperature, and the fuel to air ratio.

All this information helps the mechanics and the drivers set the car up for what will hopefully be the perfect winning lap.

The data is downloaded to a laptop for further processing by the pit crew.

When conditions are wet and dangerous, the system lets the crew know how the car is performing, enabling the driver to better handle the conditions.

DIDYOUKNOW?

GO-KART GO!

In a go-kart, you have a greater sensation of speed than in an ordinary vehicle because you are much closer to the ground. How fast you go depends on the type of kart, the length of the track and the class you are racing in. Race speeds can be anywhere from 32-160 km/h. Karts were created in the USA in the 1950s post-war period by airmen, as a way to pass spare time. Kart racing has since spread to other countries and is now popular in Europe.

Kart racing is seen by many as a fairly safe way to introduce drivers to more advanced forms of motor racing.

RACING CARS

ThrustSSC streaks past official observers as it breaks the land speed record.

Land speed records are carried out in huge, flat areas — usually deserts.

The supersonic car

In 1997 Andy Green, a 35-year-old Royal Air Force fighter pilot from the UK, drove the ThrustSSC at an amazing 763 mph or 1228 km/h in the Black Rock Desert, Nevada, USA. The car, the most powerful ever built, was powered by two Rolls Royce jet engines. It was 16.5 metres long, 3.7 metres wide and weighed 10.5 tonnes.

Not only did he set a new land speed record, he also travelled faster than the speed of sound (1,226 km/h). This was the first time the sound barrier was broken on land. Before this, speeds greater than the speed of sound had only been possible in flight.

American contenders for the world record are working on a car called the North American Eagle in the hope of smashing the record held by the British.

Is the Phillips-head screwdriver really named after a Mr. Phillips?

Yes, it definitely is! Henry F. Phillips, of Portland, Oregon, in the USA, invented the head screw and screwdriver for car makers who needed a screw that could be driven with more torque (meaning it could rotate with greater force) and that would hold more tightly than slotted screws. Car makers also needed a screw that would centre quickly and easily, and could be used efficiently on an assembly line.

The invention was initially rejected, but eventually accepted by the American Screw Co., who in 1936 persuaded General Motors to use the Phillips-head screw in manufacturing Cadillacs.

Phillips lost the patent to his invention in 1949, yet the screw is used for all kinds of jobs today.

Phillips-head screw and screwdriver.

a Phillips screwdriver and a standard flathead screwdriver

Phillips-head screws

Tools you would find in a mechanic's workshop

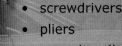

- screwdrivers
- pliers
- wrenches (box end and open end sets and a combination set)
- socket set
- sprocket set
- soldering gun
- drills
- grinders
- crimpers
- hi-tech electronic testing equipment and computers
- hacksaw
- grips
- jacks and hoists (to lift cars and engines)
- lathes
- computerised testing equipment like voltmeters and ammeters

wrenches — box end

wrenches — combination set

wrench — open end

pliers

screwdrivers

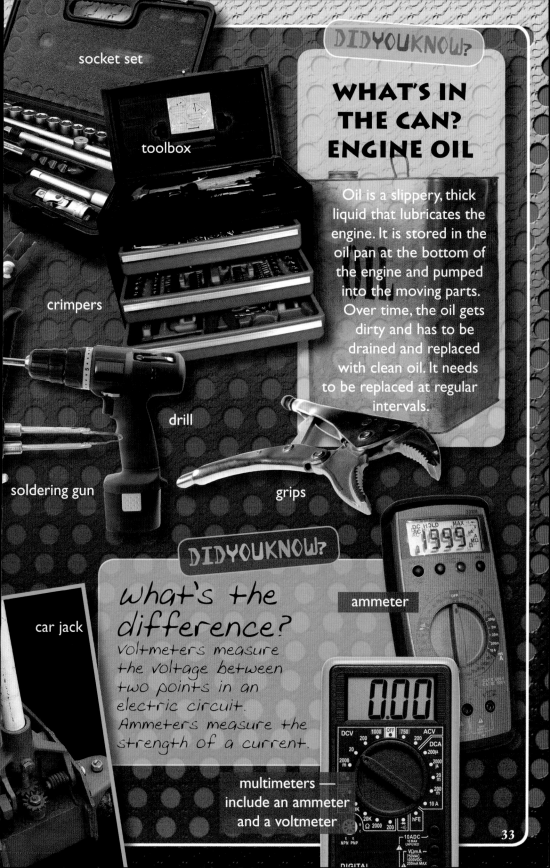

socket set

toolbox

crimpers

drill

soldering gun

grips

car jack

DIDYOUKNOW?

WHAT'S IN THE CAN? ENGINE OIL

Oil is a slippery, thick liquid that lubricates the engine. It is stored in the oil pan at the bottom of the engine and pumped into the moving parts. Over time, the oil gets dirty and has to be drained and replaced with clean oil. It needs to be replaced at regular intervals.

ammeter

DIDYOUKNOW?

What's the difference?

Voltmeters measure the voltage between two points in an electric circuit. Ammeters measure the strength of a current.

multimeters — include an ammeter and a voltmeter

33

Kart racing or karting

Many of the best professional racing car drivers started their careers through kart racing as teenagers. It is the perfect starting place for anybody interested in motor racing because the speeds are not as fast as other types of motor racing and it's generally not as dangerous.

Go-karts are exciting to drive. In karting, competitors race around a smaller-sized track. There are professional races, but there are also lots of tracks where people can go karting for fun or just to drive as a hobby.

In racing, karts are classified according to the size of the engine. Officials, called scrutineers, inspect and weigh the karts before and after the race to make sure they are in good condition and meet the requirements for racing.

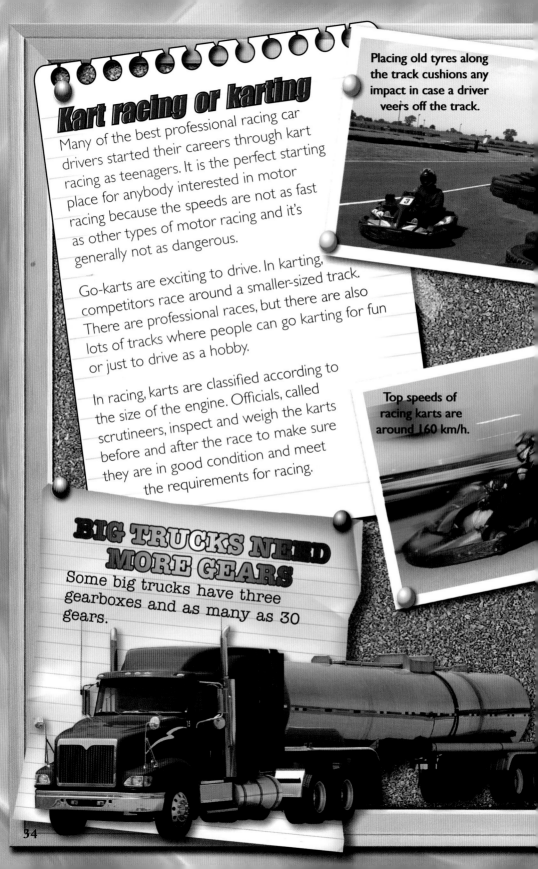

Placing old tyres along the track cushions any impact in case a driver veers off the track.

Top speeds of racing karts are around 160 km/h.

BIG TRUCKS NEED MORE GEARS

Some big trucks have three gearboxes and as many as 30 gears.

To keep the karts safe and performing at their best, I check each motor thoroughly, and also check the karts for the following:

- ☑ cracks
- ☑ loose bolts and fasteners
- ☑ frayed, weak or faulty cables
- ☑ worn brake pads
- ☑ worn tyres
- ☑ faulty pedals
- ☑ worn wheel bearings
- ☑ cracked steering rods
- ☑ kinked cables
- ☑ loose exhaust
- ☑ leaking fuel and tank line
- ☑ bent tyre rims
- ☑ worn chains and sprockets.

Cracks in the body of the kart need to be repaired to prevent further damage.

Replace damaged tyre rims.

The main components of a go-kart are a fibreglass body, seat, steering wheel, frame, engine and wheels.

steering wheel

fibreglass body

seat

wheels

frame

wheels

engine

Heavy vehicle technicians

Some technicians specialise in heavy vehicles, such as lorries, trucks, buses, military vehicles and large vans. It is a more physical job than working on cars as components are much larger to lift and manoeuvre.

Heavy vehicle technicians may work for garages, but many of the jobs are with firms owning fleets of vehicles, such as bus companies, heavy goods distributors or haulage companies. The Armed Forces train their own technicians to work on troop-carrying vehicles and tanks.

the stub axle on Josh's kart needs replacing

Most of the work tends to be preparing vehicles for their MOT and routine servicing. There are regular safety checks to be made – for instance, on fluid levels in hydraulic brake systems, oil levels and tyres. When parts fail, a heavy vehicle technician (unlike a light vehicle technician) is more likely to repair than to replace them, as parts can be very costly. In order to test-drive heavy vehicles, you need a large goods vehicle (LGV) licence.

Parts work

Parts staff look after the hundreds of different items needed to keep vehicles on the road. They have to be able to trace the part needed for a particular model of a vehicle and issue it to garage workshops or direct to members of the public.

The job usually involves ordering, invoicing and sales work. Good communication and computer skills are important.

Motorcycle maintenance

The motorcycle industry is relatively small, although it has grown in recent years. Opportunities for training and working as a motorcycle technician, however, are limited. Training positions may be available with motorcycle dealers and with a few garages, mainly in the larger towns.

It's estimated that there will be 1 200 million cars on Earth by 2030.

The problems created by too many cars include traffic jams and pollution.

CAR MAD!

There were approximately 590 million cars in the world in 2002. That's one for every 10 people. There were 140 million cars in the United States and 55 million in Japan. This contrasted with just 9 million cars in China and 6 million in India.

Raring to go?

Motorsport has a reputation for being a demanding industry to work in but it can be a very rewarding career! The race teams have high expectations so it's important that the team they employ has the right skills and training.

Young people who wish to work in the motorsport industry as a race mechanic should enrol on a full-time race-technician course. A one-year course will cover the main skills required for the industry, such as:

- race car preparation
- TIG welding
- machining
- communication
- health and safety.

You may even get to race with associated race teams as part of the course.

Next step...

Your next step is to approach race teams to become a Race Technician Apprentice. You may learn with a professional racing team and then continue on to an Advanced Apprenticeship which will last about two years full time.

Other routes in

Entry requirements are usually at a high level. Some students often take the route of A level exams and university courses.

WHAT ELSE COULD I DO?

Road rescue organisations: qualified and experienced entrants are provided with training in breakdown and recovery work by motoring organisations such as the AA and RAC. Besides technical knowledge, patrol staff have to communicate clearly with the control centre and with customers. Some weekend, evening and night work is expected. You may also train with road rescue organisations through an Apprenticeship or Advanced Apprenticeship in roadside rescue and recovery.

DID YOU KNOW?

Your skills and experience as a motorsport mechanic can take you anywhere. There are plenty of opportunities to work in other countries.

packed toolbox ready to go

With the changes in automative technology, there are now more electronic controls and computers fitted to the vehicles. As a result, there are opportunities to specialise in these areas.

Vehicle engineers work on the design, development and production of the millions of cars, lorries, vans, buses and other vehicles on our roads. Professional engineers have degrees or equivalent qualifications. There are also opportunities at technician level for those with four good GCSEs.

Major vehicle manufacturers employ thousands of people in the UK. The main centres of vehicle manufacturing are in the Midlands, Oxford, Swindon and the north-east.

PROFESSIONAL ENGINEERS

Professional (chartered and incorporated) engineers are responsible for the design, testing, development and production of a company's products. Producing a motor vehicle is a team effort. Every component has to be designed, tested and modified before it is ready to be made in quantity. Most of the design work is carried out using CAD (computer-aided design). This helps designers to work in 3D, looking at designs from all angles.

Degrees are available in automobile, automotive, mechanical and even motor sport engineering. Degree course requirements vary so check what you need with the individual colleges. Usually GCSEs followed by three A levels, a BTEC National or an Advanced Diploma are needed.

TECHNICIANS

Technicians do a wide range of highly-skilled and specialised jobs. These include assisting with:

- engineering design
- systems control
- vehicle testing and development
- quality control
- production process planning
- technical sales
- service and technical buying.

Technicians need four GCSEs at grades A*–C (or equivalent), subjects to include mathematics, English, and science. They are trained by a combination of on-the-job training and college study. Advanced Apprenticeships, leading to at least NVQ level 3, are available. Other approved work-based learning routes or equivalent qualifications are available.

CHARTERED ENGINEERS

Chartered engineers work at the highest level of research and development, planning, designing and managing projects.

INCORPORATED ENGINEERS

Incorporated engineers are often team leaders, supervising technicians and craftspeople.

Follow these steps to become a motor mechanic

1. Training programmes for young people – mainly Apprenticeships and Advanced Apprenticeships – are run by approved training providers, such as training organisations or motor manufacturers. These are available for work with light and heavy vehicles, motorcycles and for training as a motor-electrician.

2. There are no set entry requirements for apprenticeships, but employers generally look for some GCSE passes, including maths, English and science, or equivalent qualifications. Training leads to NVQ level 2 through a mixture of experience gained in the workplace and training at a college or training centre. This usually lasts for two years.

3. If you want to do an Advanced Apprenticeship many employers look for GCSEs at grades A*–D in maths, science and English, or equivalent qualifications. Exact requirements vary from employer to employer. Training leads to NVQ level 3. Advanced Apprenticeships usually last up to three years.

4. Some employers may support apprentices to continue learning through a Higher National qualification or a foundation degree. The Apprenticeship may involve training (perhaps for a few weeks at a time) at the manufacturer's own training centre to learn how to service and repair particular types of vehicle.

5. Alternatively, you may do a full-time college course. There are courses leading to BTEC First qualifications in vehicle technology, BTEC National qualifications in vehicle repair and technology, and City & Guilds qualifications in vehicle maintenance and repair at levels 1–3. Entry requirements for college courses vary from a good general education through to GCSEs at grades A*–C. Check individual course requirements in college prospectuses or on websites.

6. Some employers and colleges use assessment tests to help choose the most suitable applicants. For entry onto an Advanced Apprenticeship you often have to complete written assessments in numeracy, literacy, problem–solving and mechanical comprehension.

- Once qualified, you may be able to gain further specialised qualifications, such as those offered by vehicle manufacturers. It may even be possible to go on to a higher education course in automotive engineering.

- Promotion can be to supervisory and workshop management posts, and then possibly into general management in the motor industry. There are also opportunities for self-employment and for overseas work.

- Wages vary from employer to employer. Pay for trainees starts at around £10,000 and progresses with experience. Bonus schemes, overtime pay and company allowances can increase pay significantly. Workshop managers with main dealerships can earn £30,000+ a year.

- Both sales and technical staff who show ability and commitment can progress to management posts in the industry, but those with business and management degrees are also recruited – especially by the larger motor vehicle companies.

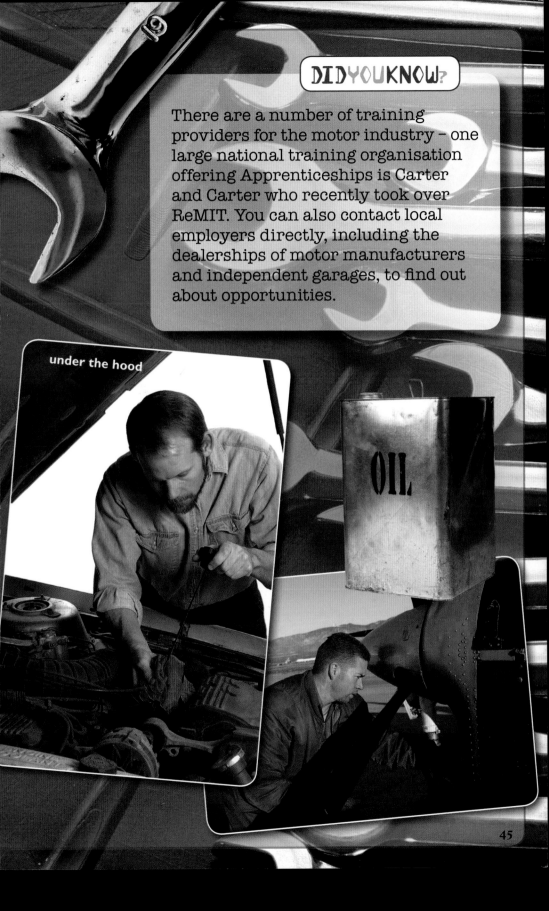

DID YOU KNOW?

There are a number of training providers for the motor industry – one large national training organisation offering Apprenticeships is Carter and Carter who recently took over ReMIT. You can also contact local employers directly, including the dealerships of motor manufacturers and independent garages, to find out about opportunities.

under the hood

OIL

Glossary

apprenticeship — learning a skill by receiving on-the-job training and attending related classroom instruction at college

brake fluid — fluid used in a car's brake system to transmit pressure to the braking mechanism near the wheels

brake pads — pads that apply friction to both sides of the brake disc

caliper — device on disc brakes which holds the brake pads

coolant — mixture of water and antifreeze circulated through the engine to carry off heat produced by the engine

dashboard — panel located under the windscreen, containing indicators and dials such as the fuel gauge and speedometer

exhaust pipe — pipe used to guide waste exhaust gases away from a controlled combustion inside an engine

fuel injector — electronically controlled small valve that controls the amount of fuel entering an engine

fuel system — system that delivers fuel to the engine, consisting of a fuel tank, fuel filter, fuel pump, and fuel injector

generator — machine which converts the power from a piston engine into electricity

jumper leads — leads used to start a car without power by conducting electrical current from one car battery to another

lug nuts — nuts that hold the wheel onto a vehicle

pinion — toothed wheel usually made of steel with a small number of teeth

piston — cylindrical piece of metal that moves up and down inside a cylinder

rack — bar with teeth on one side to mesh with the teeth of a pinion

radiator — part of the vehicle through which the coolant flows to be cooled

rotor — disc-shaped part of a brake assembly

spark plug — creates the spark in the combustion chamber of the engine, igniting the fuel and air mixture

suspension system — system of springs and shock absorbers used to suspend avehicle's frame, body and engine above the wheels

Useful contacts, books and websites

Automotive Skills Ltd - 4th Floor, 93 Newman Street, London WIT 3DT. Tel: 020 7436 6373. Careers helpline: 0800 093 1777. Provides careers information on the motor industry. In partnership with The Independent, publishes the magazine Career Driven twice a year. Also produces AutoCity, an interactive CD-ROM, through which you can explore the industry and career options. *www.automotiveskills.org.uk/careers*

The Institute of the Motor Industry - Fanshaws, Brickendon, Hertford SG13 8PQ. Tel: 01992 511521. A leading awarding body for motor industry qualifications. Oversees the Automotive Technician Accreditation scheme. *www.motor.org.uk*

There is a range of training providers for the motor industry - the following is one of the largest: **Carter and Carter Group Plc** - Mere Way, Ruddington Fields Business Park, Ruddington, Nottinghamshire NG11 6JZ. Tel: 0115 945 7200. For information on automotive Apprenticeships, tel: 0870 606 1936, and to apply for an Apprenticeship online, see: *www.carterandcartergroup.com*

Skills for Logistics - 14 Warren Yard, Warren Farm Office Village, Milton Keynes MK12 5NW. Tel: 01908 313360. The Sector Skills Council covering LGV driving. *www.skillsforlogistics.org*

A useful website for anyone considering a career in the logistics industry is *www.careersinlogistics.co.uk*

Road Haulage Association (RHA) - Roadway House, 35 Monument Hill, Weybridge, Surrey KT13 8RN. Tel: 01932 841515. *www.rha.net*

For all kinds of information about the motor industry, see: *www.autoindustry.co.uk*

For information on **the National College for Motorsport**, phone 01536 419580 or view: *www.nc4m.ac.uk*

Index